Not Really,

but

Thank you.

(I think.)

Lynn Murrell

Not really, but

ISBN-10: 1534676473
ISBN-13: 978-1534676473

DEDICATION

This volume is dedicated to Neil Howe:
sometime grouch, often genius, always loved.

CONTENTS

Not really, but

Why and Wherefore

When I was a small child, with bad hearing and worse eyesight, I learned to read. The written word opened up a world where I could understand without the need to hear. My imagination could see things so much more clearly than my eyes could see the world around me.

From then onward, I have loved words, and the worlds they can create.

The purpose of this slim volume is to share a glimpse of one of my little worlds. This world, and this project would never have seen the light of day without the encouragement of teachers - Miss Howard, Mr Parker, Miss Cooper— friends and family too numerous to mention, and more lately, my beloved Goof and the lovely folk at the Travelling Acoustic in Almeria, Southern Spain.

A truly heartfelt thank you to you all.

Not really, but

Hamlet, Prince of Denmark

Hamlet had a sorry life.
His Mum was now his uncle's wife
(Not quite the thing, especially if
your Dad is only just a stiff.)
And then his dear departed Dad
appeared to say 'Your uncle's bad.'
The wicked Claudius had done
his brother in to get the throne.
The thought of what his uncle did
nearly unhinged the poor old kid.
So thoroughly confused was he,
'To be', he mused, 'or not to be?'

While telling Mum her man's felonious,
he accidentally kills Polonius.
As if things weren't bad enough,
he's now upset his bit of stuff
(Polonius was Ophelia's dad)
and she, poor girl, goes raving mad.
A little later she is found,
bouquet in hand and rather drowned.

Laertes, who's her next of kin
decides to do poor Hamlet in.
Hamlet's demise is now assured:
there's poison on Laertes' sword
and Claudius, the rotten fink,
has put some poison in his drink.
One way he'll die, if not the other.
Unfortunately Hamlet's mother
drinks the drink and promptly dies,
much to everyone's surprise.
Meanwhile, Hamlet and his foe
have both got scratched, so down they go.
Before the Prince of Denmark snuffs it,
he takes the poisoned sword and stuffs it
into Claudius – somewhat gory.
The cast's all dead, so ends the story.

Herbicide

I found a little maggot in the cumin
I felt that it should not be there at all.
To smack it on the head would be quite human
or to squish it with a swatter on the wall

But I found that I just simply couldn't do it
as it lay there, panting, gasping for its breath,
so I put it with the pepper in the cruet
and listened while it sneezed itself to death.

A dilemma I am unlikely ever

to face

If you found a million pounds, what would you buy?
I'd inform the police, I'm sure. At least I'd try.
After a month unclaimed, I'd get it back.
They'd make me sign, and then pass me the sack
of dosh. I'd thank them very much,
then leave, the cash held in a vice-like clutch.

On my way home I'd buy some pants and socks,
a chicken and a larger letter-box
for my front door, for all the begging mail.
I'd mean to tell them no, but I would fail.

Then the serious business would begin.
I'd ponder long, my hand cupping my chin.
A robot vacuum cleaner is a must
and a flying thing to rid the place of dust
Not sure the latter's been invented yet,
but if it had, that's something I would get.

I'd pay the mortgage off. At last I'm free!
Rescue a donkey, have a cup of tea.
But what of larger things? A super yacht?
No thanks, I think I like the one I've got.

Down to almost the last nine hundred thou,
I'd worry, thinking, "What do I do now?"
I'd buy things for my kith and for my kin
and things for them to keep the presents in.
A bike for every nephew, every niece,
my siblings would acquire a car apiece.

I'd throw a party and invite my chums
and get the dog the opposable thumbs
she's always wanted, and a little friend -
a special one, with bottoms at each end.
But that's enough of me. Over to you.
If you found a million pounds, what would you do?

Ted with a bucket on his head

Who bashes and crashes and splashes about?
Who knocks over wine racks when he goes out?
Who bruises our legs with his blundering on?
Who just can't see where his dinner has gone?
Ted
with a bucket on his head.

Who waggles his four legs around in the air,
flashing his bits that are no longer there?
Who is even more than the usual pain?
Who could be quite bright, if he had half a brain?
Ted
with a bucket on his head.

Who grins with a flollopy lollopy tongue?
Who hasn't a clue what on earth he's done wrong?
An Olympic standard, gold medal twit
but terribly sweet, and we love him to bits?
Ted
with a bucket on his head.

The Epic Tale of Horatio the Lemming and his Quest for True Love

You can always tell Horatio,
'cos everywhere he goes
he leaves little furry paw prints
made by little pigeon toes.
But the reason for his charm,
as almost everyone agrees
is his great protruding teeth
and his fearfully knock-knees.

Horatio the Lemming is a charming little chap,
though his eyes are always crossed
and his big ears always flap,
but sadly that's all passed,
and I'll tell to you the saga
if you pull up close your chairs
as you sip your halves of lager.

When our hero was first born
the midwife thought that he was dead.
Well, that might have been much better,
but he went and lived instead.
He wasn't all that weak,
but then he wasn't all that strong

and everybody hoped he wouldn't be around that long.
They thought he'd jump a cliff
and get a-splattered on the shore
and their hopes weren't all that cruel,
because that's what a lemming's for.

But Horatio had better, bigger things planned
for his life:
he'd sail the seven seas
and then seek fame and find a wife.
But one could tell by looking at him,
didn't need a second glance,
our poor misguided hero just didn't stand a chance.
But he set off, nothing daunted,
saying 'Just you wait and see!
I'll be back with just the perfect little lemming lass for me.'
So he took off with his toothpaste
and his brush in his rucksack
with a smile upon his face, and the bag upon his back.

Well he wandered far and wide
until he saw upon a hill
a sight that made him catch his breath
and made his heart stand still.
'This is the one I've dreamed of,'
he muttered with a sigh
He set off up the hill – his hopes were running high.

'Oh Madame, I think I love you!
I will not be denied.
Oh Lovely Lemming Maiden,
I must have you for my bride!'
But the lovely lemming maiden seemed as though she hadn't
heard.
She sat there, quite immobile
and she never said a word,

which is really not surprising
– I beg you do not laugh –
our poor myopic hero poured his heart out to a scarf.
He pleaded with her feebly,
thought his heart would break in twain,
then swore he'd never chase after a woolly scarf again.

For days he wandered back and forth,
not knowing where to go.
The unsuccessful courtship had really laid him low,
but at last he saw a sight
that made him giddy with surprise.
She was ravishing and stunning.
He could not believe his eyes.
He fast removed his spectacles
– they weren't very cool—
then he swaggered to the lady
and pretended not to drool.
In no time at all he'd fallen for her charms
and he was smitten.
Unfortunate Horatio was falling for a mitten.

He brought her roasted worms to eat,
and spiders for her tea
But his ladylove was silent,
and not a word said she.
His heart was overflowing
and her love was all he yearned
Poor Horatio, all unknowing, by a mitten he was spurned.

Eventually he realised he had not one single friend.
He decided life was rotten,
so he'd bring it to an end.

'I'll do just one thing right,'
he thought, a-lying in his bed.
'I'll catch the train tomorrow
and I'll go to Beachy Head.'
So the next day in the morning,
just as soon as it was light,
he set off to do the one thing
that he thought he could do right.
And by quarter past eleven,
although he was scared stiff,
the broken-hearted lemming was standing on the cliff.

'Farewell to you cruel world,
and all that is in you!' he wept,
and pinching tight his runny nose,
he closed his eyes and leapt.

As he fell, his life flashed before
his sad and weary gaze -
the tragedies and heartaches that his death would soon
erase,
like the time I didn't mention
when his hopes were crushed quite flat,
when he found that for six years
he had been chatting up a hat.

And as he thought of all the sad events
he'd left behind,
a hand dragged him from the water,
and a voice that sounded kind
said, 'Well mate, you were lucky that we chanced to be
around.
You could have hurt yourself, you know.
You might have even drowned.

But then again, I guess it's quite
unlikely that you could -
you seem to float quite well because your leg is made of
wood!'

'Oh cruel, cruel fate!' he cried,
'You should have let me be.
I hoped to drown my sorrows,
and intended to drown me!'

The captain of the ship was filled
with sorrow and remorse.
He'd done what he thought best,
and he had only made things worse,
and, thinking that the lemming wouldn't wish to be ignored,
he grabbed him by the tail
and quickly threw him overboard.

'I'll shoot myself!' he muttered,
as he drifted to the shore,
with his tail stuck out behind him,
and his leg afloat before.

So he bought himself a gun
and with a savage little grin
he went to find a quiet spot, to kill himself therein.
He wandered through a forest,
where he found a leafy glade.
'This is just the perfect spot', he thought,
'for committing suicide.'

So he stood beneath the trees,
his gun was pointing to his head,
when a perfect lady lemming clutched his elbow and she
said,

'Oh please, most handsome lemming,
this is not the thing to do –
I have waited all my life
to meet a lemming such as you,
and I know within my heart
that I just couldn't bear the pain
if I met you briefly once
and then my love was gone again.
Oh please, my Darling Lemming,
I beg you, don't despise
the love of this poor maiden.'
tears were brimming in her eyes.

OH RAPTURE, BLISS and ECSTASY!!!
Away flew all his fears.
He took her in his arms,
her words still ringing in his ears.
He whispered lovely nothings
and she whispered them right back.
Their joy was all complete.
They were in love. But oh alack,
as to take her for a cuddle in the leafy glade he led,
the gun went off within his hand
and shot her in the head.

'My Love, my sweet, I've shot you!'
Horatio he cried.
He held her in his arms,
and with a broken heart he died.

The moral of this story,
laid down for you in verse
is 'However big your problem,
it will probably get worse.'

An ode to my love

Ambrosia of Albion's sweet pasture!
Elixir of youth, oh hear my plea!
Oh how I long to clutch thee to my bosom,
to gaze upon, and to partake of thee!

So long I've waited, panting, sighing, yearning -
a whole eternity it surely be!
The flame of my desire is always burning -
I just can't wait to have a cup of tea.

Dog hair, feathers, dust

We live in Spain, my love and me,
in blessed and blissful harmony
with a small menagerie.
We're broke, but we're not fussed.
We have each other to delight,
the sun by day, the stars by night
and just three things the joy to blight:
dog hair, feathers, dust.

I fight with bucket, mop and broom
to keep them out of every room.
Friends chuckle at me. They assume
that I shall soon adjust,
but cleanliness is what I need
and so I pay them little heed.
I'm busy with the tumbleweed
of dog hair, feathers, dust.

My love comes whistling through the door.
He kisses me, I kiss him more
then other stuff – you know the score –
we're overcome with lust.
But suddenly my passion's choked.
His isn't, but then, he's a bloke.
My OCD flares at a stroke
from dog hair, feathers, dust.

"But what's the problem?" he will say
"You cleaned up only yesterday.
It doesn't matter anyway."
I know that. But. It's just
it very slightly bothers me
my latent control freakery
when drifting round the room I see
dog hair, feathers, dust.

But life is great. It's no big deal
and underneath it all I feel
no longer on the hamster wheel
of grinding out a crust.
I'm free to do what pleases me:
enjoy my life, my family
indulge in fancy cookery
or read a book, or learn to ski,
or take up re-upholstery
or scuba, darts, or topiary
and maybe pay for somebody,
instead of me, bi-annually
to rid the house, my love and me
of dog hair, feathers, dust.

She was only the chiropodist's daughter

She was only the chiropodist's daughter
but she wasn't a callous girl.
She fell in love with the confectioner's son
who got her in a whirl

But he was in love with the gardener's girl
and she was all for lawn,
for her desire was the lawyer's son-
undying love she'd sworn.

But the lawyer's son was a bit of an oath
who loved the chiropodist's daughter.
He pursued her in his skin tight briefs
and one dark night he caught her.

She was only the chiropodist's daughter
and could surely smell de feet,
so she fended him off with a corny excuse
and a promise that they would meet.

Now the banker's son loved her from afar.
He'd kept his feelings in cheque,
but his patience at last went overdrawn
and thinking "what the heck!"

18

he asked the girl to marry him,
but she'd married the tripe-dresser's son,
who'd had the guts to ask her first.
My story's almost done,

but just one thing I've left to tell.
their kids' names were such fun ones:
a bouncing pair of baby twins
called little Tripe and Bunions.

Those good ol' menagerie blues

Old Ma Murrell had a house, E I E I O
and in that house she had a man E I E I O
With a lost sock here and some lost specs there,
here a book, there some glue,
get the picture? Yes we do.
Old Ma Murrell had a house E I E I O

Old Ma Murrell had a house E I E I O
and in that house she had a dog E I E I O
With a dog bowl here, and an old bone there,
here a ball, there a toy
dog hair shedding everywhere,
here a book, where's the glue?
You've moved my trainers, haven't you?
Old Ma Murrell had a house E I E I O

Old Ma Murrell had a house E I E I O
and in that house she had a bird E I E I O
With a "Pretty Boggle!" here, and birdseed there
here a tweet, there a song, good job they both get along.
Dog bowl here, old bone there,
suspicious looking object down the side of the chair,

here a book, there the glue
I haven't had it, must be you!
Old Ma Murrell had a house E I E I O

Old Ma Murrell had a house E I E I O
and in that house she had a duck E I E I O
With some duck poo here and some duck poo there,
down and feathers floating through the air,
"Pretty Boogle!" here and whistling there,
loud dawn chorus ringing through the air,
dog bowl here, old bone there,
Oh no! Not again! She must be eating hair!
Rubber gloves, bleachy mop, when will all the
madness stop?
Here a soldering iron (yes really) Where's my beer?
CDs and song-sheets up to here.
Old Ma Murrell had a house E I E I O

Old Ma Murrell had a house E I E I O
and in that house she had a tiny abandoned puppy
(This is getting ridiculous!) E I E I O
with a piddle puddle here and a piddle puddle there,
trip-hazards underfoot everywhere,
quack quack here, duck poo there,
cockatiel song ringing through the air.
Dog bowl here, old bone there,
empty fridge and ironing piles everywhere.
Where've you put the car keys and my clean
underwear?

I think I've lost the plot, and I don't know if I care!
Old Ma Murrell had a house **E I E I O**

The Great Vegetable plot of 1509

Gather round, ye merry throng
of noble heart and stomach strong
I'll tell a tale both tall and long.

In the year 1508
(1509 would have been too late)
a crown was put on Henry's pate.

Now Henry was a merry King -
you'd often hear him gaily sing
as he chomped his way through anything

you cared to serve. He couldn't stop.
He caught his wife out on the hop
and sent her off to get a chop.

He'd eat a roast boar in one go.
Huge banquets he would often throw,
with heaps of rich food, all for show.

To satisfy his massive greed,
he'd guzzle buckets full of mead.
His gut complained. He paid no heed.

His gluttony made others fret.
The leftovers were all they'd get.
His selfishness bred disquiet.

Because his manners were not good,
his courtiers thought him rather rude.
Yet more disgruntled was his food.

While Henry scoffed yet more and more,
downstairs in the vast food store
council was being held — of war.

"I can't think how we can fight back,"
said a turnip on the rack.
"This vegicide can't be ignored.
Maybe we could get help abroad."

"Yes!" cried a seedy looking fennel,
"Let's call our friends across the channel!
Our pals upon Le Continong
will help us fight this dreadful wrong.
For a diplomatic show of muscles
let's contact our sprouts out in Brussels!"

The spuds said "Do you think that's fair?
We're King Edwards, so we don't care,
but once you've let these foreigners in
they might not go back home again."

"Well really! How could you be so narrow-
minded?" asked a large, ripe marrow.
"Besides, there's a lovely young courgette,
a French cousin I've never met.

If we could persuade her to come over,
I'd meet her off the boat at Dover."

A red-faced betroot pushed him aside.
"British vegetables!" he cried,
"While you just sit around and natter
King Henry's paunch grows ever fatter.
Vegetables of the world, unite!
Let's get to war! Let's stand and fight!
Our allies from Italy, Spain and France
may be our one and only chance."

Three minutes later, towards Calais
a runner bean was on his way
across the Channel. A one man Navy,
he rowed in a boat that was made for gravy,
stolen from the Royal pantry.
He rowed to save his friends and country.

Meanwhile, hiding underground,
the Résistance was to be found.
"An English bean 'e 'as been seen,"
Muttered a stringy-looking bean.
"I sink we murst investigate,"
he said, pulling his beret straight.
"Our French Olympic runner bean must go
-send Sebastian's cousin, 'Arry Coe"

That midnight, 'neath a moon so bright,
one could espy the strangest sight:
a quiet allotment full of veg,

watching the English bean signing a pledge
not to divulge the whereabouts
of the secret army of onions and sprouts,
radish and radish and baby beets,
(I said radish twice, because radish repeats)
and rank upon rank before his eyes,
veg of every shape and size,
row upon row, drill upon drill,
every last one of them licensed to kill.

"What eez thees problem what you 'ave got?"
enquired a smartly dressed carotte.

He told them of his friends who died
to satisfy the King's inside.
The sentimental onions cried.

"Oh! Zut alors! Je ne comprend pas!"
cried one after another petit pois.
(Their stupidity is why one sees
so much thick soup is made from peas.)

"You peas don't need to understand."
The carrot had the whole thing planned.
"We'll get the info that we need
from our undercover agent Swede.
We planted him in England a year ago -
he'll tell us all we need to know."

"That really is an awful joke!"
guffawed a jovial artichoke.
"Planted him a year ago!
Hehe! Haha! Hehe! Hoho!"
The silence killed his laughter off.
He gave a small embarrassed cough.

"Your joke so malo it make me ill!"
moaned an orange from Seville.
"I'd throw the little idiot out,"
griped a rather sour Kraut.
"Gott und Himmel! Vas ist das,
zis artichoke should be so crass?"

"Don't-a you think-a we ought-a to know
what we're-a going to do-a before-a we go?"
asked an Italian tomato, turning red.
"Ah bon! Of course!" the carrot said.
"I 'ave a plan," he said with a smile.
"Mes chers amis, écoute a while."

Back in England's merry land,
King Henry, with a cake in hand,
had all official fasting banned.
And to celebrate, the greedy beast
ordered the biggest ever feast.

That night in bed poor Henry dreamed
a nightmare warning, so it seemed.
A giant spud with visage grim
said it would be the death of him,
that if the King did not behave,
he'd soon sleep in an early grave,
a victim of cholesterol
sent to plague his mortal soul.

The Monarch made a hasty plan.
He was a very frightened man.
He'd give up food (except for bran.)

But Henry was a fickle bloke,
and in the morning when he woke
he gave himself a little treat
and tucked into three Shredded Wheat.

"Where is my Lord Chamberlain?"
he cried. They brought the courtier in.
"I want a giant feast tonight,"
he said "Make sure you get it right."

The scene changes now to later that day.
The party was getting underway.
Everyone sat in his place.
The King intoned a hasty grace.

While licking his lips King Henry sat,
the chef brought in a boiling vat.
"For your pleasure and delight,
a stew for you, oh Sire, tonight!"
he cried, "I'd be most honoured if
the Royal nose would take a sniff."

The King remembered last night's dream.
He knew that face, or so it seemed.
His uneasy feeling was overcome
by a mighty rumble of his tum.

He leaned over the vat, to see if it would
be good enough for the royal pud.
As he leaned, a huge hand, far from kind
pushed his amply round behind.
"HAHA! We've got you now, old thing
you gluttonous, greedy, obese King!
It's time you got your fair come uppance.
Yell all you like - we don't care tuppence!"

And as Henry gave a gurgling scream,
he knew the face from last night's dream.
The erstwhile spud, dressed as a chef
smiled as Henry gasped for breath.
Worse than the worst he'd ever feared,
the carrots grabbed hands full of beard
and pulled him ever closer to
the surface of the roiling stew.
The vegetables snarled and frowned
and smirked and leered. The King just drowned.

I'd like to say that he repented,
that the undercover spud relented,
that the episode transformed his life,
he lived to take another wife (or four)
but I can now reveal to you
he died, the victim of a stew.

So when you read he died of gout,
you'll know a misprint is about-
for 'gout' you probably should read 'sprout.'

And when you read your history books,
remember things weren't how it looks.
Forget the lessons of your youth:
I tell you now the awful truth
Henry VIII, poor old soul,
was murdered, by a casserole.

Advice for animal lovers

Don't have a pet centipede
although the idea may seem nice.
Affection is not in their nature
and they're only one step up from lice

Don't have a pet centipede.
There are much better pets you could choose.
Their bedding and food costs are minimal
but think of the price of the shoes.

And another thing

My pet aversion's ironing.
I have a growing pile
of shirts and shorts and sundry stuff,
all wrinkly, dry and vile.

Cleaning the loo is ghastly too,
dog sick is my bête noire -
I just abhor it slightly more
than hoovering the car.

I dislike airports, slugs and snobs.
I can't stand passive smoke.
I don't like things too chocolatey.
I don't like being broke.

I can't stand loud and leery drunks,
the egocentric bore
who feels the need to tell me things
he's said ten times before.

I don't like yoofs with motorbikes
or Mr Tony Blair
or avocadoes, flies, B.O.
unwanted facial hair,

solicitors who stitch you up,
repeats on BBC,
vegetables overcooked,
or sugar in my tea.

I loathe shopping, beetroot stains,
athlete's foot and wasps,
Nazis, people who are smug
and things that don't quite rhyme.

Bossy wimmin drive me nuts.
Long queues are a pain,
but the thing that gets me most of all
is people who complain.

On the demise of my favourite pants

I never felt the need to make a song
and dance about them, as you would a thong.
They were just there. No frills and fancy frippery,
no brazen silk seductive, smooth and slippery
no floral prints, cute logos, bits of tulle;
just cotton, somehow cosy, somehow cool.

Washday would come, I'd hang them on the line,
embarrassed by their workmanlike design.
Among the other, flimsier, netherwear,
they'd waft discreet; you'd hardly see them there.
And we both knew, my underthings and I
that they were pants on which I could rely.
I'd fold them, smooth them, tuck them in their drawer
the front row, like a thousand times before,
while silky sulking, huddled at the back,
impulse buys in purple, red and black.

I knew deep down that there would come a day
for reason, cold and sensible, to say,
"They've had it. They're worn out, elastic spent.
They're disreputable. Time they went."

Faded fighters, somehow they soldiered on,
thumbholes each side, elastic nearly gone.
I loved those pants with passion and profundity,
secure in my custodians of rotundity.
Desperate, I dyed them, hoping to delay
decomposition that came anyway.

Today, with grieving heart, the Rubicon
was crossed. I'm here. My favourite pants are gone.
But not too far. A sort of immortality
conferred upon them by extreme frugality.
In the midst of death they are in life! My plants
are tied with my beloved underpants.
Each strip of cotton tied with gentle fingers,
nestling amidst green life, their presence lingers.
Somehow recycling mollifies the grief;
I smile at blooms with bloomers, leaves with briefs.

Think yourself lucky!

Folk like you need telling,
so I'll put the record straight.
Those who spend their whole life smelling
don't enjoy a happy fate.

It's not an easy life, you know.
It's not a bed of roses.
I'll never, ever have a wife
I'm not surprised. I spose it's

because I'm always smelling.
I smell. There now! I've said it!
My Father smelled before me
you could call it heredit   ary.

All I do is breathe and smell.
It just can't be denied
because I am a nose, you see,
with nostrils either side.

Don't get me wrong – I wouldn't pick
this kind of job, no, never.
It's rather antisocial
and it isn't even clever

34

It's not really the sort of thing
that's glamorous to do.
You wouldn't choose my kind of job
if you'd the choice, would you?

Just be grateful, Ladies, Gents,
you're not like me accurst.
Oh well, I could have been a foot
and then I'd smell much worse.

A winter's tale

The bed is warm and womblike,
your feet like buttered toast,
when beneath the covers comes the call,
the thing you dread the most.

You've only just defrosted
and dropped off, or so it seems,
and now contrary innards
have disrupted your best dream.

Your brain is slow to surface:
it tries to stay submerged
within the arms of Morpheus,
ignore the primal urge.

The sea bass you were eating
on the island, in the sun,
with the hunk you were convinced this time
might really be The One,
for reasons you can't quite work out,
is now swimming in the loo,
has grown arms, and hands and fingers,
and is beckoning to you.
You try to shift position, move a leg, gyrate a hip,
adjust a pillow, anything to give the urge the slip.

You want to sleep, perchance to dream
of shoes and chocolate cake,
but your body is determined
and it wants you awake.

Your other half, meanwhile,
is sleeping peacefully and tight,
hands crossed on his bosom
like some medieval knight.
To wake him would be degenerate,
dastardly, a crime.
His prostate isn't acting up. Not yet, but give it time.

You lie there, twitching gently,
not to wake the slumbering one,
as your bladder shouts admonishments
of what you should have done.
'I thought I had,' you mutter,
'just before I cleaned my teeth.'
but your bladder turns a deaf ear,
as it screams for swift relief.

Eventually the torture is too much.
With a sigh you ease a toe
in the general direction
that your bladder wants to go.
Stifling a gasp, you put your foot upon the icy floor;
an act that aggravates your inner urges even more.

Better to grab a dressing gown, or to eschew delay?
You go for speed, teeth chattering,
as you rush on your way.
No time for slippers, spectacles,
lights or clothes for you,

as naked and myopic you go dashing to the loo.
The porcelain is icy: now your poor rear is as well.
Can you get frostbite in your cheeks?
Only time will tell.

Returning to the hollow
that still holds your body heat,
you feel sensation creeping
down your legs into your feet.
Your mind begins to wander
as you gently drift away
and ponders things that make no sense
but wonders anyway:

Are lemons good for goldfish?
Can seed potatoes wink?
Is Captain Kirk a Hindu? What do alligators think?
What happens if a caterpillar
finds it needs a wee?
Does it struggle from its chrysalis and suffer, just like me?

A waste of space

There are four things
in all the world
that no-one seems to need:
wasps are one
appendixes
Donald Trump
and weeds.

The Ballad of Mad Marcel

Ce soir, for you, Mesdames, Messieurs,
the story I will tell
how Mad Marcel Marsupial
built La Tour Eiffel.

Now, Mad Marcel Marsupial, the Parisian kangaroo
was fiddling with his pouch one day
with nothing better to do.
He scratched himself upon the head
and hopping round said he,
"I'll build, pour moi, an Eiffel Tower
so the word will remember me."

"Oh, Arc de Triomphe! Place de l'Étoile!
Hôtel des Invalides!
Zis will be the greatest pièce de ré-
sistance ever did!"

So he gathered ten tons of rivets
and a couple of jars of glue,
several miles of ironwork
and a master plan he drew

singing, "Sacré Coeur! Gare St Lazarre!
Montmartre! Notre Dame!
Zis will be the greatest building known
to kangaroo or man!"

For months he laboured at his task.
The people cried mockingly,
"Qu'est-ce que c'est que ça zis Marcel builds,
zis overgrown wallaby?"

Oh, Champs Elysées! Bois de Boulogne!
Place de la Concorde!
No mattered how they mocked
his progress couldn't be ignored.

It grew so tall, it grew so fine,
by kangaroo leaps and bounds.
He was growing so excited
his feet barely touched the ground.
He ate his garlic sandwiches as he worked -
he wouldn't stop.
When the last joint was mitred, he was so delighted
he hopped right off the top.

Oh, Airport Charles de Gaul! Rive Gauche!
Centre Pompidou!
That enormous hop from off the top
Was the last he'd ever do.
Oh, défense de fumer! Bateau Mouche!
Toilette Municipal!
To this hour the tower's a monument to
Marcel Marsupial.

So as you go drifting down the Seine
you know what you must do:
Shed a silent tear for Mad Marcel the Kangaroo.

Prequel

You don't get to choose who you love, they say,
but some types of love aren't allowed
and things can get ugly where prejudice reigns
and a mob lurks within every crowd.

They were star-crossed lovers, mixed race freaks,
a pair where a pair should not be,
in a world where the *other* must always be feared
and the fettered believe they are free.

A session musician, he held down three jobs,
while she laboured in pest control
and they loved, how they loved! with a love strong and deep
but a love not allowed to be whole.

As long as they kept their affection well hid,
as long as they played by the rules
they could carry on quietly with their lives.
The charade of indifference was cruel.

Weekends were a bittersweet time of romance.
Stolen kisses were urgent and few.
Repression and ignorance girdled their world
but love bloomed there, radiant and true.

"Can't we just run away, be together?" she'd cry
at their clandestine trysts in the park.
"Trust me, we shall, and soon my love."
His tenderness guarded the spark

of a dream of a world where their love could be free,
with denial and pretence stripped away.
They saved their pennies and stockpiled food
preparing, they hoped, for the day.

At last, she wrapped up their money and food
in a waterproof, new five pound note
and the owl and the pussycat sailed away
in a beautiful pea green boat.

TED

My eyes, unseeing, closed,
first lay dreaming in the cradle,
while, milky-lipped and swaddled and separated,
my body drifted in sleep
you were there.

When speech was understood, but yet unformed,
when roses on the walls were faces
that leered and shifted,
by my side, speaking silent comfort,
close and reassuring,
a world of warm acceptance
you were there.

A new surprising triumph
cheered on by my brother,
while mother hovered anxiously close by,
and every step a gleeful
almost accident.
Watching and approving,
you were there.

Clutching you upon the dining table,
all uncertain, dimpled knees and elbows,
brushed and primped for an unscheduled caller
who persuaded her to have me pictured,
you were there.

Through the first broken heart
and countless relocations,
then sat with Poo Pah as the years sped by,
watching my own children
as your contours changed
you were still there.

And then through separation
and depression and despair,
life almost too broken and fragmented
even to attempt to fix the remnants back together
you were there.

You with your saggy bottom,
beady eyes and crumpled face,
your neck unable to support your dear head,
propped by a hook around one ear
you're still here.

And when I am no longer,
other arms will hold you
that knew you all their life and know your worth.
And while I go on ahead,
leaving them behind,
you'll be there.

Not really, but

ABOUT THE AUTHOR

Lynn Murrell appears on the surface to be a rather dishevelled person, who likes animals and people more than she likes housework. She is well-known for her love of tea – "builders' brew, just a splosh of milk, please" and her propensity for napping.

Well hidden beneath the indolent facade is a mind constantly in overdrive, a fertile imagination and an affection for the offbeat, the strange and the, frankly, ridiculous.

Not really, but

Thank you. (I think.)

17544384R00033

Printed in Great Britain
by Amazon